Thoughts and Feelings

Thoughts and Feelings

Jealous

Written by Sylvia Root Tester
Photos by David M. Budd

The Child's World®, Inc.

Published by The Child's World®, Inc.

Design and Production:
The Creative Spark, San Juan Capistrano, CA

Photos: © 1998 David M. Budd Photography

Library of Congress Cataloging-in-Publication Data

Tester, Sylvia Root, 1939-
    Jealous / by Sylvia Root Tester.
        p. cm. — (Thoughts and feelings)
    Includes bibliographical references.
    Summary: Simple rhyming text describes jealousy, how it feels, and
what can cause it.
    ISBN 1-56766-671-X (lib. bgd. : alk. paper)
    1. Jealousy in children Juvenile literature. [1. Jealousy.]
I. Title. II. Series.
BF723.J4T47 1999
152.4'8—dc21

99-28175
CIP

6

I'm up in my room.
I've banged the door.

My face feels all red,
I'm kicking the floor.
The trouble is this:
I'm jealous you see.
Everyone here is ignoring me.

That baby's to blame,
my new baby sister!
Everyone that I know
wants to hug and kiss her!

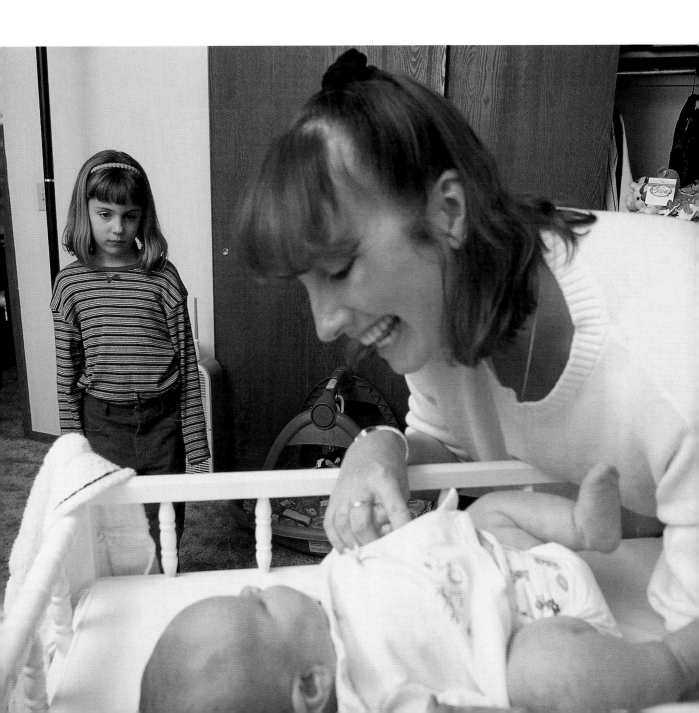

She's got my old room.
My little bed, too.
My mom's always cuddling her
because she's so new.

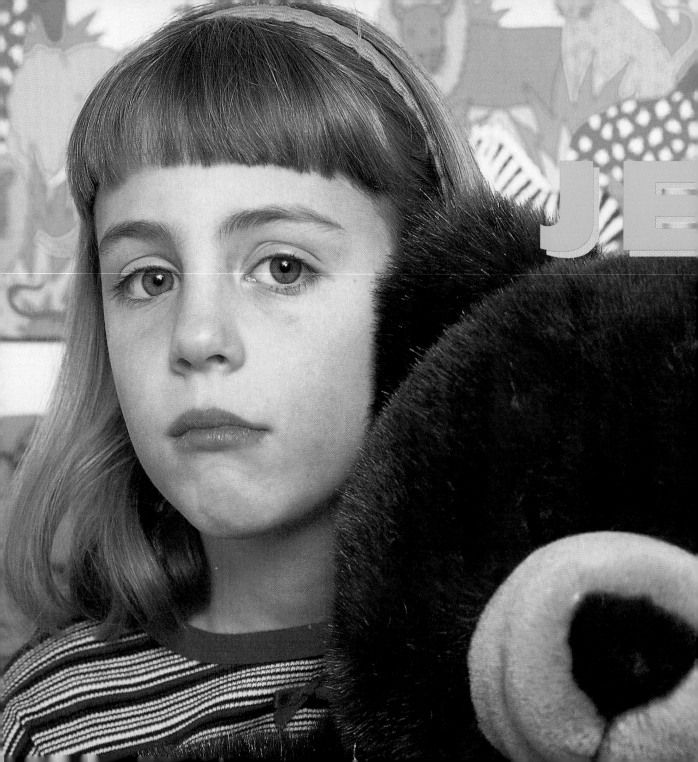

JE

Have you ever been

JEALOUS?

It doesn't feel right.
You want to kick
and scratch
and bite.

15

I've been jealous before.
Oh yes, indeed!
I was jealous when Laura
learned how to bead,
and I couldn't do it.

But then I learned, too.
I found out it wasn't
so hard to do.

I was jealous when my
friend got a kitty—
until I got a dog.
Now isn't she pretty?

Here is my Aunt Rachel,
knocking at my door.
She wants to see the
new rug on my floor...

23

and my big, new bed,
and the paint so white.

My dad did the painting.
He did it just right.

Mom baked my favorite cake last night!

And Daddy bought
me a brand new kite!

29

I guess being jealous
isn't so smart.
There's still room for me
in everyone's heart.

For Further Information and Reading

Books

Amos, Janine. *Jealous.* Austin, TX: Raintree Steck-Vaughn, 1991.

Cristaldi, Kathryn. *Samantha the Snob.* New York: Random House, 1994.

Aaron, Jane, and Barbara Gardiner. *When I'm Jealous.* New York: Golden Books, 1998.

Web Sites

For more information about thoughts and feelings: http://www.kidshealth.org/kid/feeling/

Fairy tales and stories about thoughts and feelings from all over the world: http://www.familyinternet.com/StoryGrowby/